his p'
the c
and h
peopl

Now if you've seen *Black Panther*, you know that the picture, for all its merits, does not present a particularly radical political vision. It shows Black people as capable of grea. t feats of intellect and physical strength, and the builders of a great civilization, but also accepting of established social order. T'Challa even has a white CIA friend who—in contrast to all of colonial Africa's history—actually wants to help for benevolent reasons. Granted, it's only a movie. But if you compare *Black Panther* with the pictures of the time that truly did assert a radical vision—*The Battle of Algiers, Nothing but a Man* (Malcolm X's favorite film) Melvin Van Peoples's *Sweet Sweetback's Baadasssss Song* (Huey Newton's favorite film), and especially Sam Greenlee's *The Spook Who Sat by the Door*–this Disney/Marvel concoction is lacking in radical vision. And this is reflected by how many people found themselves identifying with the ostensible bad guy Killmonger, rather than the ever-polite, if uber-competent, titular hero.

Now this isn't to attack *Black Panther*. In a time when so many negative images of Black culture—

men and women—exist across the media, there is something to be said for the representation shown in the picture. Images are important. When Richard Pryor spoke in the 1980s about a trip to Africa, he observed the regal beauty of the women and the inherent dignity of the men—something he had not seen growing up in Peoria. "My eyes was full, Jack," he says, with evident emotion. And he resolves in front of an audience to stop using "that word"—the N-word—because when he looked out at the sea of people he didn't see any N-words there. Pryor didn't stick to that resolution, for other reasons, but the point is that Black people deserve their cultural heroes just like anyone else. It's just that, by political standards, T'Challa doesn't rise to the level of Foxy Brown or John Shaft, much less Dan Freeman or Sweet Sweetback.

To understand what happened to the Black Panthers, part of the answer lies in a culture that regards *Black Panther* as "radical." It's the same culture that regards Bernie Sanders as a revolutionary leftist when in fact he's a moderate liberal. The hardcore right-wing in this country have been so successful in dominating the media that people had forgotten what the left is supposed to look like.

BLACK PANTHER
PARTY

A LONG TRAIN OF ABUSES

"It comes as a great shock to see Gary Cooper killing all the Indians, and although you are rooting for Gary Cooper, to find that the Indians are you." —*James Baldwin*

Although many white people don't like to hear about it—hence the success of Fox News and the existence of Trump voters—it is almost impossible to overstate the horrifying effects of slavery and institutional racism in the U.S. Far from ancient history, the legacy still clouds everything in this country. The 15th Amendment, allegedly guaranteeing African-Americans the right to vote in 1870, proved so toothless that it wasn't until the 1965 Voting Rights Act—*almost 100 years later*—before *some* of the major blockades were removed. And that's only one small part of racism's all-pervasive influence.

One example of how racism distorts everything occurred in the spring of 2017. Donald Trump met with the Congressional Black Caucus. Trump was told that reforming welfare would be unpopular with the caucus' constituents, "not all of whom are Black." To which Trump replied, "Really? Then what are they?"

The statistics clearly show that there are far more white people on welfare than Black. But in general, people *associate* welfare with Black poverty. Donald Trump is a soulless, empty sack of white supremacist shit, but in this case he was thinking like most Americans.

For generations after the Civil War, little progress was made in race relations, as Black citizens were trapped in their status of second-class citizens. However, during World War II, Black Americans fought alongside white Americans against the Nazi threat, achieving some level of forced assimilation. Returning soldiers understandably felt disappointed about resuming the former civil structures that reduced them to second-class citizens. As Langston Hughes put it in "Beaumont to Detroit: 1943":

> *I ask you this question*
>
> *Cause I want to know*
>
> *How long I got to fight*
>
> *Both Hitler—and Jim Crow.*

Slow, symbolic achievements were made. In 1947, the Dodgers broke the color line in starting Jackie

Robinson, who would quickly become the most exciting player in the league and one of the greatest second basemen of all time. In fact, the fading of the perpetual dominance of the New York Yankees in the 1960s would be a result of their reluctance to scout Black players. Meanwhile, in the 1950s, Sidney Poitier and Dorothy Dandridge broke into pictures and became stars; and Harry Belafonte became the first solo artist of any color to sell a million copies of a record, *Calypso*, in 1956.

The Jim Crow laws (enforcing segregation) were repealed in 1954. This led to further violence against Black churches and individuals, particularly in the South. In 1955 in Mississippi, fourteen-year-old Emmett Till was lynched for the crime of allegedly whistling at a white woman. In addition to which there were many more violent incidents and outright murders committed after the dissolution of the Jim Crow laws. (Hollywood would later dramatize some of these events in a film called *Mississippi Burning*, in which a heroic FBI agent played by Gene Hackman saves the day for Black America. Needless to say, the FBI were on the side of the Klan, not people of color.)

As Robert F. Williams documents in his classic *Negroes with Guns*, the escalating series of atrocities against Black people in the South kept tempers high. Even the NAACP leadership, with its mission of peaceful education, worried about a violent insurrection from within its own ranks. Writing about an ugly incident in North Carolina, Williams pointed out that armed self-defense prevented a massacre: "There is only one reason why the racist mob lost its nerve in their projected attack against the Negro community. Knowing as they did we were well-armed, they found it impossible to stomach the thought of violence." Surrounded by hostiles and unprotected by law, armed self-defense proved an appealing survival option for Black people.

Then came the escalating situation in Vietnam.

Ten years after these incidents, in March of 1965, began Operation Rolling Thunder, a series of bombing attacks across North Vietnam that would go on for the next three years. A month later in April, a civilian student protest in Washington, D.C. attracted 15,000 participants. This was four years *before* the draft started. By June of 1966, there were over 300,000 American troops in Vietnam and the U.S., for the first time, began bombing Hanoi, the Northern capitol.

The great boxer Muhammad Ali (formerly Cassius Clay) spoke for many when he said, "Why should they ask me to put on a uniform and go ten thousand miles from home and drop bombs and bullets on brown people in

Vietnam while so-called Negro people in Louisville are treated like dogs and denied simple human rights?"

Meanwhile, in March of 1965 Dr. Martin Luther King led a five-day march from Selma, Alabama, to the capitol steps in Montgomery, Alabama. Together with a group of nonviolent demonstrators, Dr. King and the Southern Christian Leadership Conference (SCLC) and the Student Nonviolent Coordinating Committee (SNCC) covered 54 miles to protest, among other things, the notoriously violent racist Selma Sheriff Jim Clark. King also aimed at putting pressure on President Lyndon Johnson, who had gotten the Civil Rights Act passed in 1964 in the wake of John Kennedy's assassination.

After the group's arrival at Montgomery, King told the crowd that it was not an accident that the march was taking place in that Southern state. Montgomery, he said, had been the first confrontation (referring to the Rosa Parks bus incident of 1955), but further battles had been fought throughout the south, and particularly in Alabama:

> But not until the colossus of segregation was challenged in Birmingham did the conscience of America begin to bleed. White America was profoundly aroused by Birmingham because it witnessed the whole community of Negroes

> facing terror and brutality with majestic scorn and heroic courage. And from the wells of this democratic spirit, the nation finally forced Congress to write legislation in the hope that it would eradicate the stain of Birmingham. The Civil Rights Act of 1964 gave Negroes some part of their rightful dignity, but without the vote it was dignity without strength.

Really, there's no way to do justice to how bad life was in the South for Black people during this time, and in some ways little has changed. But no matter how bad you think it was, it was worse. It wasn't enough to be segregated, to grow up in devastating poverty, with no prospects for a future life of independence. You also knew that if you stepped out of line, if you dared to look the wrong way at a white person, you might end up murdered, with no outlook for justice. The two men who killed Emmett Till were acquitted.

MALCOLM X

There was one another event that occurred in 1965—another of the important assassinations of the 1960s, although it is not often treated as such. It was the murder of Malcolm X, which took place in February of that year in New York. Malcolm had gone from Detroit Red, a street hustler, to prison, to the voice of the American Nation of Islam (NOI). Malcolm grew famous by making dazzling speeches and debating white commentators on television and intellectually crushing them. His analysis of Black-white relations in 1964 resonates to this day: "If you stick a knife in my back nine inches and pull it out six inches, there's no progress. If you pull it all the way out that's not progress. Progress is healing the wound that the blow made. And they haven't even pulled the knife out much less heal the wound. They won't even admit the knife is there."

The Nation was essentially a dictatorial organization, run by Elijah Muhammad, and when Malcolm discovered that Muhammad had sired a number of children through unwed sex with his secretaries and hangers-on, he lost the faith. He also earned many enemies within the Nation of Islam, as well as with the federal authorities who were already targeting him.

In 1964 he took a pilgrimage to Mecca which changed his attitude—no longer seeing all white men as "the devil," he grew to understand struggle as essentially a class phenomenon, and began a short career as an internationalist.

And that's how Malcolm X became one of the most dangerous men in America. His removal from the NOI, although it brought many hardships, *freed* him; he became a general ambassador to the oppressed world. He embodied resistance to the Genghis Khan morality of mass capitalism.

Malcolm decided to bring evidence of America's racial crimes before a United Nations tribunal. For his trouble, the FBI wiretapped his plans and, recognizing their potential global impact, the FBI shared the information with the Department of Defense, military intelligence, and the CIA. As Malcolm had embarked on a world tour of sorts, traveling to meet Castro in Cuba and with Saudi Arabian royalty, among others, the FBI followed him along every stop. Attorney General Nicholas Katzenbach sent a memo to J. Edgar Hoover suggesting at one point that Malcolm might be prosecuted under the Logan Act (an act that stipulates ordinary citizens as unable to make treaties on behalf of the U.S. without authorization.) In a sense this underscores the incredible nature of Malcolm's personal stature—greeted as a foreign dignitary at every spot, and tracked by a U.S. government that recognizes his extreme level of threat, despite his lack of resources.

His murder was also a conspiracy—and although we won't go into it this issue, there are resources available provided at the end where you can find out the whole story. However, Malcom is important because so much the 1960s can be seen as fulcrum swinging between MLK and Malcolm and, indeed, they were moving in a direction towards one another when each man was murdered by the state.

In terms of activist politics, however, Malcolm's death left a void that would be filled the next year by the BPP. The NAACP, SNCC, and SCLC were all doing important work, but for young people faced with an increasingly violent situation on the street, more direct action was needed.

ENTER THE PANTHERS

Into that void stepped the Black Panthers. Unlike previous organizations such as the various MLK-associated groups, they did not embrace nonviolence but rather self-defense; unlike the Black Muslim movements they embraced a return to Africa.

The story of the Black Panther Party, unlikely enough, begins with a place called Kaiser Aerospace and Electronics. A young ex-Air Force technician and engineer, Bobby Seale, worked on engine frames for the Gemini missile program. In 1962 Dr. Martin Luther King came to the Oakland auditorium to give a speech and Bobby was one of the 10,000 people there that day. When Seale first told me that it was Martin Luther King who had inspired the BPP, I was surprised. But he said the inspiration came from his realizing the power of numbers. Imitating MLK's speech and delivery patterns, Bobby recited: "We're gonna boycott Wonder Bread. We're gonna boycott them so consistently and profoundly we wanna make Wonder Bread wonder where the money went." He was so energized by that speech that he decided to give up on engineering and

go straight into organizing. In fact, he said MLK's legacy is "more special" to him than the legacy of Huey Newton or Eldridge Cleaver. His idea was always to organize businesses: "First we democratically unite the small businesses in communities and second...we also start up businesses that are non-profit, managed and actually owned by all the workers."

Bobby had been organizing with other civic entities in the Oakland area—quite successfully, working with the local mayor's office among other things—when he met Huey Newton. Huey, he learned, had been ransacking people's cars at Herrick Hospital! He needed the money. Bobby told him, "Huey, you can't be pulling no crap like that." So he hired him as an assistant in 1965.

Huey would go on to become the main face and voice of the Black Panther Party. He would also go on to obtain a doctorate (his Ph.D thesis was called *War Against the Panthers*) and would use overtly Marxist theory and language in his communications. Theoretician Huey and organizer Bobby got the Panthers off the ground.

Over the course of the next several years, many important figures in the Panthers emerged: Eldridge and Kathleen Neal Cleaver, Elaine Brown, Elbert Howard (who recently died on July 27, 2018), H. Rap Brown, Fred Hampton, Bunchy Carter, Geronimo Pratt, George Jackson, Ericka Huggins, David Hilliard, and Mumia Abu-Jamal.

In addition to these, there have been some Black Panther Party members that achieved fame later. The singer Chaka Khan, actor Samuel L. Jackson, and musician/songwriting genius Nile Rodgers all were party members at one time. TV personality Judge Joe Brown was even a member of the Panthers. It is extraordinary, especially because there were so few registered members.

Another startling thing I learned from Bobby Seale was that the BPP, at its height in 1968, had only about 400 members across the country. For a group of such critical importance in history, it was incredibly small. They were mostly along the West Coast, including a

Sacramento office that was all female (about 60% of all BPP members were women), as well as Portland, Seattle, Chicago, and few cities in the East. And yet several of those went on to achieve great success in their chosen professions. Bobby himself had been an engineer on the NASA Gemini program before he dropped out to organize full-time.

A list like this can only trace the major incidents in a handful of individuals, but everything mentioned in these pages will reward further study from the resources at the end.

BLACK PANTHER PROGRAMS

The Black Panther Party was a party of programs. If you follow the logic that an occupying force governed the ghettos—that is, white supremacy—then it made sense to offer community programs. And of course, anyone who makes any effort to check will find out that Black communities traditionally have the worst of services. Even now, calling the police has a level of danger for a person of color that simply does not exist for most white people. But beyond that, from voting machines to medical care, nothing worked as it should. As Flavor Flav of Public Enemy said, "I'll call a cab 'cause a cab would come quicker," in the song "911 is a Joke."

The BPP set up public health clinics, called the People's Free Medical Centers. These provided screenings, shots, and blood pressure exams to the public. Other programs included youth education and free breakfasts for children, the idea being to break the hold of white supremacy at the source. There were also free food programs and a community newspaper. All of these programs, in addition to helping the people through direct action, tended to make the BPP

COMMUNITY DISCUSSION GROUPS

WOULD YOU LIKE TO HAVE A MEMBER OF THE B.P.P. COME TO YOUR HOME AND DISCUSS:

1. •The Ten-Point Platform and Program of The BLACK PANTHER PARTY and What it Means To Black People,
2. •The Need For COMMUNITY CONTROL OF POLICE.
3. •The Need For Black People To Become REGISTERED VOTERS So They Can Sit on Jury Panels and Give Justice To Black People.
4. •The Murders of FRED HAMPTON and MARK CLARK in Chicago.
5. •The Many Attacks on our Homes and Offices in L.A., CHICAGO, NEW YORK. etc. and The International Harrassment, Repression and Murders of The Members of The BLACK PANTHER PARTY.

HOME DISCUSSION GROUPS SHOULD NUMBER AT LEAST SIX PEOPLE. APPOINTMENTS ARE AVAILABLE BETWEEN THE HOURS OF 9am & 7p.m., SEVEN DAYS A WEEK.

CALL-
BERKELEY – 845-0103 or 0104
E. OAKLAND – 568-3334
SAN FRANCISCO – 922-0095
RICHMOND – 237-6305

ALL POWER TO THE PEOPLE
BLACK PANTHER PARTY Nat'l. Hq.
3106 SHATTUCK AVE. BERK.

very popular. They had stepped in to fulfill what the government had decided not to follow through on.

Perhaps the most unlikely location for a BPP chapter was Portland, an overwhelmingly white city. And yet a group that started with less than ten people eventually beganto maintain free health clinics in 1968, and dental clinics starting in 1970. Despite little funding and zero support from the government, those services were maintained in various forms until 1979 and were adopted by the State of Oregon as a variant of single payer healthcare.

What the BPP had was a ten-point program:

1. *We Want Freedom. We Want Power To Determine The Destiny Of Our Black Community.*

2. *We Want Full Employment For Our People.*

3. *We Want An End To The Robbery By The Capitalists Of Our Black Community.*

4. *We Want Decent Housing Fit For The Shelter Of Human Beings.*

5. *We Want Education For Our People That Exposes The True Nature Of This Decadent American Society. We Want Education That*

Teaches Us Our True History And Our Role In The Present-Day Society

6. We Want All Black Men To Be Exempt From Military Service.

7. We Want An Immediate End To Police Brutality And Murder Of Black People.

8. We Want Freedom For All Black Men Held In Federal, State, County And City Prisons And Jails.

9. We Want All Black People When Brought To Trial To Be Tried In Court By A Jury Of Their Peer Group Or People From Their Black Communities, As Defined By The Constitution Of The United States.

10. We Want Land, Bread, Housing, Education, Clothing, Justice And Peace.

LEAVE IT TO THE CLEAVERS

The Black Panther newspaper was started by Huey Newton in April of 1967. Quickly, one of the most important writers for the paper emerged: Eldridge Cleaver.

Cleaver, who became Minister of Information for the BPP and worked as a journalist for the leftist muckraking magazine *Ramparts*, achieved a literary reputation through writing the classic *Soul on Ice* in 1968. This book is unlikely to ever be embraced again by liberals, as it's intensely provocative. Cleaver opens by explaining that as a young man he deliberately raped white women as a political act. If you can get past his admission—and recognition that what he did was wrong—the book is often brilliant. It is as informed by Jack Kerouac's *On the Road* as it is by Frantz Fanon.

Eldridge was so notorious that the Oakland police set him up for execution. They showed up at a house he was staying in and fired machine-gun bullets and tear-gas into it in early 1968. The Panthers inside returned fire, as they promised to do, and the standoff lasted some 90 minutes. Eventually he, along with Little Bobby

The BLACK PANTHER

BLACK COMMUNITY NEWS SERVICE

VOLUME 1 APRIL 25, 1967 NUMBER 1

P.O. BOX 8641 OAK. CALIF. EMERYVILLE BRANCH

PUBLISHED BY THE BLACK PANTHER PARTY FOR SELF DEFENSE

WHY WAS DENZIL DOWELL KILLED

APRIL FIRST 3:50 a.m.

"I BELIEVE THE POLICE MURDERED MY SON" SAYS THE MOTHER OF DENZIL DOWELL.

Brothers and Sisters of the Richmond community, here is the view of the family's side of the death of Denzil Dowell as compiled by the Black Panther Party for Self Defense, concerned citizens, and the Dowell family. As you know, April 1st, 1967, Denzel Dowell (age 22), was shot and killed by an "officer of the Martinez Sheriff's Department",

Hutton, who was a seventeen-year-old BPP member, walked outside the house with their hands up. Hutton stripped to his underwear to prove he had no weapons. The Oakland police opened fire anyway and murdered Hutton in cold blood, shooting him twelve times, while also wounding Cleaver.

Kathleen Neal Cleaver, who married Eldridge at the end of 1967, stayed with him for some twenty years, living in Algeria, and starting an International Chapter of the Black Panthers there.

Kathleen earned a law degree from Yale and continues her work to this day in various organizations. Despite the large number of women in the party and successes like Kathleen Neal, life as a woman in the BPP could be difficult. Elaine Brown, who became an officer in the BPP in 1974, wrote that the men often behaved misogynistically within the ranks. In her book *Taste of Power*, Brown wrote: "If a Black woman assumed a role of leadership, she was said to be eroding Black manhood, to be hindering the progress of the Black race." In this way the organization mirrored the society and was not as progressive as one would have liked. Still, Elaine became the first woman to lead the organization in 1974.

Another woman who also went on to accomplish a great deal, especially in the context of prison reform, is Angela Davis. Although primarily she was attached to the USA Communist Party and only for a short time with the BPP, Davis found herself a fugitive from the law. Some guns that Davis had purchased wound up in the hands of Jackson, a teenager, who pulled out the weapons in a Marin County, California courtroom. In a police shootout that occurred as Jackson was attempting to escape with three other Black men,

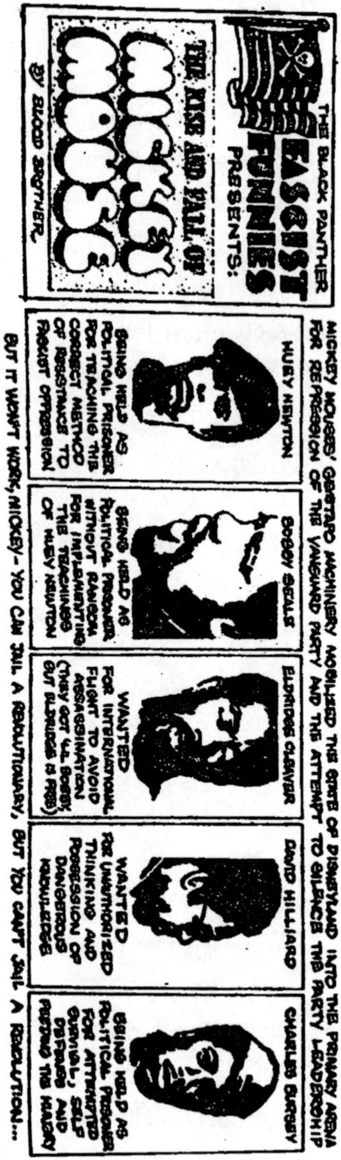

the judge was shot twice and killed. Davis was picked up under California conspiracy statutes.

Davis, in her brief period as a fugitive, appeared on the FBI's 10-most wanted list, and received notoriety as a result of President Richard Nixon referring to her as a "dangerous terrorist."

In the 1971 trial for which Davis was eventually found innocent, she was defended by Communist Party lawyer John Abt. (Abt is also notable as the lawyer mentioned by name by Lee Harvey Oswald when he requested a defense in the assassination of John F. Kennedy.) After her acquittal, Davis would go to teach at the University of California Santa Cruz, running the Feminist Studies department.

COINTELPRO AND THE "SNITCH JACKET"

The Panthers, like any large political action group, did not operate in a vacuum. Their outward displays (carrying guns in public and promising self-defense against the police) came as a response to a system that brutalized Blacks as a matter of course. The FBI and the Justice Department did not sit still and watch these "second-class citizens" protest against what they saw as the rightful order of things. They went into action.

From the earliest agitation came COINTELPRO, J. Edgar Hoover's investigative program aimed at putting down any new "Black messiahs." From 1956 to 1971, COINTELPRO surveilled some 20,000 people, while operating actively in a counterintelligence capacity against several thousand of those. In 1968, J. Edgar Hoover referred to the BPP as the "greatest threat to the internal security of the country."

One FBI trick was to design coloring books showing Black people committing violent acts against whites, and sending them to white liberals. The idea was to cut off sources of funding for the Panthers by pretending they were creating pointlessly violent content. The FBI knew that powerful liberals had come forward to support the Panthers; for example, the famous *West Side Story* composer Leonard Bernstein held BPP meetings in his Manhattan apartment. (How great those parties must have been is another question.)

A favorite trick of law enforcement and the intelligence services is called snitch-jacketing or bad-jacketing, making it look like someone is an undercover government operative when they aren't. The false impression seeds confusion and suspicion within the organization. Stokely Carmichael, (later Kwame Ture) was one of the most important and vocal figures in the BPP. So the FBI targeted him to be snitch-jacketed.

Carmichael had gotten the attention of President Lyndon Johnson as early as 1966. He had, among other things, gone on the program *Face the Nation* and stated that he felt Black people had no business fighting in Vietnam. A concerned LBJ ordered a report on Carmichael.

A memo dated July 10, 1968 spells out the details:

> ...consideration be given to convey the impression that CARMICHAEL is a CIA informer. One method of accomplishing would be to have a carbon copy of an informant report supposedly written by CARMICHAEL to the CIA carefully deposited in the automobile of a close Black Nationalist friend..."

The gambit worked. Huey kicked Stokely out of the BPP.

Remember, we are talking about an organization with chapters across the country, which meant that Seale and Newton had to rely on many other people for information and control. As a result, chapters were only as good as local leadership, and being that these were politically Marxist, arguably fringe groups, there were some levels of drug and crime.

As it became clear that local law enforcement and FBI COINTELPRO operations had successfully penetrated the Panthers, a paranoid atmosphere soon followed. A California BPP "field marshal" from California named George Sams, Jr., went to New York to help instill discipline in the New York office.

Alex Rackley was a 19-year member of the New York chapter of the BPP. A martial arts instructor, he was not well-versed in the complex leftist literature favored by Huey Newton and may not have fully understood what he was doing beyond helping the community. Rackley was quickly accused of being an FBI informant. When Rackley couldn't answer questions coherently, Sams was even more suspicious. Rackley was tied down and tortured for days, primarily by pouring boiling water on him. Ericka Huggins boiled the water and assisted in the torture.

George Sams ordered Walter Kimbro and Lonnie McLucas to take Rackley out to a marsh in Middlefield, Connecticut, and kill him. Kimbro shot him first, followed by McLucas.

Sams turned state's witness and testified that Bobby Seale had ordered the killing, all evidence to the contrary. After the first trial, Seale and Ericka Huggins were put on trial as well. The second trial ended in a hung jury, although the majority of the jury favored acquittal for both parties. However, the entire scene had a bad odor. Seale said at the time, "I'm just the

Chairman. I don't pay attention to everyone." Although no doubt true, it revealed some of the internal schisms and problems within the organization. And the fact of the matter was that Sams had ordered a murder in cold blood for no good reason. It was never known whether Rackley was actually an informant; indeed, considering his behavior, it's possible that Sams had been.

FRED HAMPTON

Fred Hampton became the head of the Chicago chapter of the BPP when he was 18 years old. A local NAACP youth leader from thirteen years old, Hampton was framed for the robbery of a local ice cream truck. Experiencing the "justice" proceedings first hand pushed Fred further to the left and to become involved with the BPP. A dynamic speaker, Hampton got several local programs started in the area, including a youth breakfast and education program.

However, Hampton became a target for infiltration and assassination by the FBI. William O'Neil, one of Hampton's best friends and the Treasurer of the local chapter, contracted with the FBI, having received about $17,000 from them in 1969 alone. O'Neil set up the assassination by drugging Hampton's drink before he went to bed, ensuring he would not wake when the police arrived to serve a warrant at 3 A.M. on December 4, 1969.

The police broke into the home where Hampton was asleep and came in firing, also killing Mark Clark. Hampton was shot in the back of the head where he slept. The raid was led by Daniel Groth, long rumored to have been a CIA plant. Groth also happens to be the man who arrested Thomas Arthur Vallee, a Lee Harvey Oswald lookalike, in Chicago. Groth played a key role in the Chicago Plot, one of the other murder plots against John Kennedy before he was murdered in Dallas.

The Hampton case was extraordinary because there was no attempt to disguise the details of the murder, as authorities had done with Dr. King and the Kennedys. The indefensible execution of a 21-year-old man in his bed by a bullet to the head was assumed to be sufficient, and indeed it was. In short order a panel led by U.S. Attorney General Ramsey Clark found that the police had fired first and never stopped shooting despite people inside the house begging them to cease, including a pregnant woman. This indefensible behavior, however, resulted in no action against the officers.

Fred's brother Bill Hampton continued community work in the Chicago area and we maintained occasional correspondence until his death in February 2018. At the time of his death, Bill was the commissioner of the Maywood Park District.

THE PANTHER 21 TRIAL

Following the 1970 trial of Bobby Seale, the Black Panther started to disappear as an organization. In addition to the internal problems, the COINTELPRO infiltration had been largely successful. On April 2, 1969, 21 Panthers were arrested for an alleged conspiracy to bomb and otherwise commit other terrorist acts against the police. One of the members arrested was Afeni Shakur, who in 1969 had written a series of articles designed to fool the FBI into believing the Panthers were ending.

The trial began in 1971, and largely due to her efforts, the Panther 21 won their freedom. A month after winning the case, Afeni Shakur gave birth to a baby boy she called Tupac Amaru Shakur, who would later become the hip-hop artist 2Pac.

Tupac was adopted as a young man by Mutulu Shakur, who was also targeted by COINTELPRO operations. Mutulu remains in prison to this day, having been arrested for alleged racketeering charges.

This, in addition to the politically-oriented lyrics in 2Pac's rhymes, may explain why the FBI considered

2Pac a threat for his entire life. 2Pac published articles in *Covert Action Quarterly*. Much great work on the 2Pac case can be found in John Potash *The FBI War on Tupac Shakur.* An interview I did with him can also be found on the website for the now-defunct Coalition on Political Assassinations (COPA).

THE DEATH OF HUEY NEWTON

The death of Huey Newton is another concerning example of how the Panthers were perceived. If you read a typical newspaper account of his death, it says that Huey was killed by Tyrone Robinson outside a crack house in a drug deal gone bad.

This version leaves out an important aspect of the story: COINTELPRO targeted Newton ferociously, resulting in a series of legal problems from the harassment. Unfortunately, he also got hooked on cocaine in the process; another Panther, Geronimo Pratt, stated that this was a result of FBI infiltration and an inside agent—Elaine Brown. Now Pratt himself had been a target of COINTELPRO, and he was imprisoned in 1972 for a murder he did not commit. Pratt's conviction wasn't overturned until 1997, when it was found that the prosecution had hidden exculpatory evidence from the jury. However, there was additional evidence that was tainted: in particular, a receipt signed by Elaine Brown from a paint shop that had repainted Pratt's car to match the car seen at the scene of the crime.

Pratt said that when Huey got out of jail, Brown kept him in a house and plied him with women and drugs. The habit never left Huey, who remained in a fog, in and out of trouble until the day of his death.

Still, you might say: no one forced him to take drugs after prison. The simple reality, though, is that his life was lived under constant pressure. How long would you last, knowing the FBI had targeted you for destruction? Knowing that FBI and CIA agents had infiltrated the organization you started in the hopes of pursuing change? While also knowing that government infiltrators had played key roles in the deaths of previous revolutionaries like Malcolm, Dr. King, and Fred Hampton? Put yourself in his shoes. Or in the shoes of Geronimo Pratt, who spent 27 years in jail, including eight years in solitary, after being railroaded by the prosecution and an alleged friend? Or in the shoes of H. Rap Brown (Jamil Al-Amin), who is still in prison today despite the fact that another person confessed to committing the same crime?

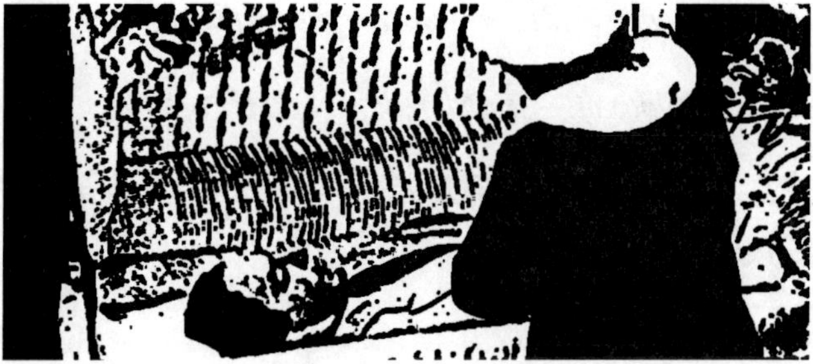

FATES OF THE PANTHERS

As you can see just from this survey of some of the principals, the Black Panthers faced political infiltration, arrest, and assassination. And that is the answer to 'What Happened to the Black Panthers?' For the most part, they were destroyed by the state. Though in many ways, members went on to leave a big impact on the world and continue their mission through other avenues. Here is a short list of some of them:

Bunchy Carter—murdered, 1969

John Huggins—murdered, 1969

Mark Clark—murdered by police, 1969

Fred Hampton—murdered by police, 1969

Little Bobby Hutton—murdered by police, 1968

Huey Newton—murdered by FBI, 1989

H. Rap Brown—framed for murder, died in jail 2011

Richard Aoki—killed himself in 2009; BPP infiltrator and police informant

Many former Black Panthers, as noted before, are still alive and active, including Bobby Seale, David Hilliard, Kathleen Neal Cleaver, Elaine Brown, Mumia Abu-Jamal (currently in prison), Mutulu Shakur (currently in prison) and Bobby Rush.

People—especially white people—often feel (or are taught) that the Panthers brought this onto themselves, or that they were somehow wrongheaded in their actions. There are always reasons to criticize any political organization, and always standards that any of us may fail to live up to, especially in hindsight. However, what needs to be understood is that the Panthers were responding to a legitimate political life-and-death emergency. In fact, their responses are only going to look more reasonable as time passes and society continues its inevitable slide into collapse. Colonialism and monopoly capitalism created the conditions for its own destruction; it's just that the Panthers were ahead of the curve.

THE LAST WORD

A few years ago I interviewed the Socialist Party member Eugene Puryear. He later became the Socialist Party Vice-Presidential candidate in 2016. Puryear has written a brilliant book about the private prison system called *Shackled and Chained.* Puryear's analysis of the system reveals that little has changed for people of color since the first birth pangs of the new nation. The old slavery has been replaced by economic slavery for those in poverty, and literal slavery for those who end up in prison. Although the Panthers no longer exist (the so-called "new" Black Panthers have no connection whatsoever to the original organization), the problems that stirred them into action remain distressingly true today. I'll give Puryear the last word:

> Going into the economic crisis of the 1970s, which was a shock because in the post-World War II period, you had these rising standards of living and the expectation—especially after the Civil Rights movements of the 60s—an expectation among Black Americans that their lives would improve, but the 1970s really upset the apple cart. The idea of jobs programs, more

> extensive social problems, all of that went to the chopping block for a variety of reasons, but you also had this other problem—particularly in the Black communities, which became the primary targets of mass incarceration—in that they were left outside the social contract, with no prospects for employment or rebuilding the communities that were being devastated. Government policy makers had no desire to help anything other than big business interests and had no desire to deal with these people in a constructive fashion so of course, the issue becomes what do we do with all these people? So that really the mass incarceration "solution" arose out of a surplus population problem. You have a group of people who have been consistently ground down, oppressed, and exploited, and at the same time you need to find a way to deal with them. Just like other forms of what is now called "neoliberalism," mass incarceration came about as a response to a structural crisis within the capitalist system.

Without addressing these core problems, political progress is not achievable.

SOME KEY FIGURES IN THE BPP

Bobby Seale: co-founder and Chairman of the Black Panther Party for Self-Defense in Oakland, CA

Huey Newton: co-founder and Minister of Defense of the Black Panther Party for Self-Defense in Oakland, CA; obtained a doctorate in social philosophy; imprisoned in 1968 for a highly controversial incident in which he was wounded and a police officer died; conviction reversed on appeal in 1970; murdered in 1989

"Little" Bobby Hutton: The first treasurer of the BPP; murdered by police in 1968

Elaine Brown: Became the BPP Minister of Information after Eldridge was expelled from the Party; later, from 1974-1977, served as the first chairwoman of the BPP

Elbert "Big Man" Howard: One of the six original members of the BPP (Seale, Newton, Hutton, plus Reggie & Sherman Forte); author of *Panther on the Prowl*

Eldridge Cleaver: *Soul on Ice* author; BPP Minister of Information and later Head of the International BPP

Kathleen Cleaver: Became Communications Secretary for the BPP after meeting Eldridge; the first female officer in the Party

Angela Davis: Communist Party member, civil rights and prison activist, was also in the BPP for a short time but was nonetheless one of its most famous members

Stokely Carmichael (later Kwame Ture): Honorary Prime Minister of the BPP; co-author of *Black Power*

H. Rap Brown: Minister of Justice in the BPP; chairman of SNCC (the Student Nonviolent Coordinating Committee)

Fred Hampton: the young head of the Chicago chapter of the BPP, murdered by police in 1969

David Hilliard: Chief of Staff in the BPP; later founded the Huey P. Newton Foundation.

SOURCES

Alexander, Michelle. *The New Jim Crow.*
Baldwin, James. *The Price of the Ticket.*
Carmichael, Stokely. *Ready for Revolution.*
Carson, Clayborne. *Malcolm X: The FBI File.*
Cleaver, Eldridge. *Soul On Ice.*
Davis, Angela. *Women, Race, & Class.*
Foner, Philip (Ed). *The Black Panthers Speak.*
Gregory, Dick. *Dick Gregory's Political Primer.*
Haas, Jeffrey. *The Assassination of Fred Hampton.*
Jones, Charles E. (Ed.) *The Black Panther Party (Re)Considered.*
Metress, Christopher (Ed.) *The Lynching of Emmett Till.*
Newton, Huey. *War Against the Panthers, To Die for the People, & Revolutionary Suicide.*
Potash, John. *The FBI War on Tupac Shakur.*
Seale, Bobby. *Seize the Time.*
Van Peebles, Melvin. *The Making of Sweet Sweetback's Baadasssss Song.*
Williams, Robert F. *Negroes with Guns.*

You can find my articles "Manning Marable's Malcolm X" and my interviews with Bobby Seale, Eugene Puryear, and John Potash in my book *Dissenting Views II.* My articles "The Open Assassination of Fred Hampton" can be found in *Dissenting Views* and also online at ratical.org. A previous Microcosm zine, *An Intro to the MLK and RFK Conspiracies: 1968* contains a full dissection of the MLK murder.

ALSO AVAILABLE IN THE CIA MAKES SCIENCE FICTION UNEXCITING SERIES FROM MICROCOSM.PUB:

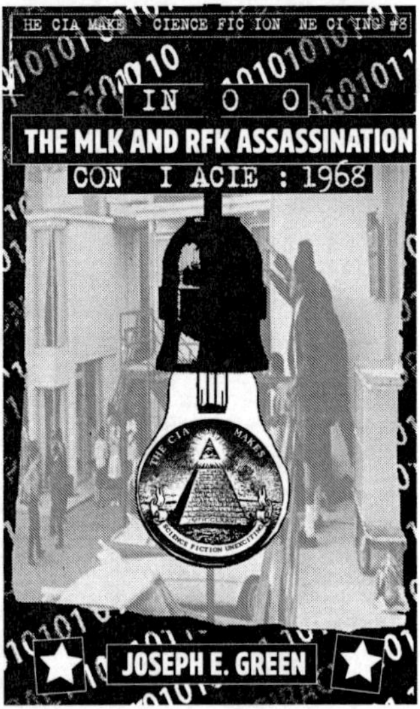

ALSO AVAILABLE IN THE CIA MAKES SCIENCE FICTION UNEXCITING SERIES FROM MICROCOSM.PUB:

This has been volume 10 in *The CIA Makes Science Fiction Unexciting* series.

Microcosm Publishing
2752 N Williams Ave.
Portland, OR 97227
www.Microcosm.Pub
(503) 799-2698

Edited and designed by Joe Biel
First Published September 15, 2018

Microcosm Publishing is Portland's most diversified publishing house and distributor with a focus on the colorful, authentic, and empowering. Our books and zines have put your power in your hands since 1996, equipping readers to make positive changes in their lives and in the world around them. Microcosm emphasizes skill-building, showing hidden histories, and fostering creativity through challenging conventional publishing wisdom with books and bookettes about DIY skills, food, bicycling, gender, self-care, and social justice. What was once a distro and record label was started by Joe Biel in his bedroom and has become among the oldest independent publishing houses in Portland, OR. We are a politically moderate, centrist publisher in a world that has inched to the right for the past 80 years.